DECCAN HERITAGE
FOUNDATION

Striving to promote and implement the preservation and
conservation of the historic monuments and cultural heritage
of the Deccan within a holistic environment and social context

Deccan Heritage Foundation Ltd
20–22 Bedford Row
London WC1R 4JS
www.deccanheritagefoundation.org

© TEXT Marika Sardar
© PHOTOGRAPHY Surendra Kumar

DESIGN Nidhi Sah
PRINTING JAK Printers Pvt Ltd

ISBN 978-81-8495-694-8
First Jaico Impression 2015

PUBLISHED BY
Jaico Publishing House
A-2 Jash Chambers,
7-A Sir Phirozshah Mehta Road
Fort, Mumbai - 400 001
jaicopub@jaicobooks.com
www.jaicobooks.com

HYDERABAD, GOLCONDA

The Deccan Heritage Foundation would like to acknowledge the generous support of **Teresa Aguirre, Maria Embiricos, Irene Moscahlaidis, Elly Sistovari and Shamina Talyarkhan** in bringing out this publication

HYDERABAD, GOLCONDA

Marika Sardar
PHOTOGRAPHY **Surendra Kumar**

JAICO PUBLISHING HOUSE

Ahmedabad Bangalore Bhopal Bhubaneswar Chennai
Delhi Hyderabad Kolkata Lucknow Mumbai

DECCAN HERITAGE
FOUNDATION

CONTENTS

12657

In the Hyderabad of today – fast-paced, high-tech, sprawling – visitors can still find traces of the gracious and aristocratic culture with which the city is associated. For those interested in learning about the history of this modern metropolis there is much to be discovered. The neighborhoods of Hyderabad's Old City are dotted with the palaces and tombs of 18th- and 19th-century aristocrats, and early 20th-century civic buildings. Visitors can plunge back even further in time at the fortress of Golconda. Though now engulfed within the western residential reaches of Hyderabad, its 14th-century citadel is well-preserved, and the 16th- and 17th-century palaces dating from the height of Golconda's wealth still stand. All of these sites and monuments are presented here.

THE QUTB SHAHIS

The region surrounding Golconda and Hyderabad has come under the sway of several successive dynasties since the 13th century, when Golconda was first built, and the 20th century, when our architectural tour ends. When constructed, Golconda functioned as a defensive fort in the western part of the realms of the Kakatiya kings (ca 1158-1323). It was one of several citadels established by the Kakatiyas or their subordinates at a time of increased military activity. This heightened level of conflict was the result of the expansionist policy of the Khilji and Tughluq sultans of Delhi, which led to a series of invasions being launched into the Deccan in the mid-12th- to early 13th-centuries. These were not successful in terms of gaining permanent territories for the Delhi-based sultanates, but the three major dynasties that had previously ruled the Deccan – the Yadavas, Hoysalas and Kakatiyas – were toppled, leaving a vacuum of power to be filled.

In their stead two major dynasties arose, the Bahmanis (1347-1538) in the northern Deccan, and the Vijayanagara kings (1336-1565) in the southern Deccan. In the 1360s, Golconda was captured by the Bahmanis from the local chieftain who had occupied the fort in the aftermath of the Kakatiya downfall. It remained a minor fort within the Bahmani realms, a part of the Telangana province of the Bahmani sultanate, at the head of which a courtier named Sultan Quli was appointed in the late 15th century. Sultan Quli Qutb al-Mulk ('Sultan' was part of his given name,) had arrived in India at the court of the Bahmani sultans at Bidar in the late 1470s. He had come to Bidar seeking refuge;

PAGES 10-11
Mahbub`Ali Khan, the 6th Nizam, and companions on a tiger shoot; photograph by Raja Deen Dayal, ca 1885 (courtesy Clark Worswick)

OPPOSITE
Inside Golconda Fort

his family belonged to the Qara Qoyunlu clan, which had once controlled large areas of western Iran but had recently been forced from power by the opposing Aq Qoyunlu clan. He found favor with the Bahmani ruler Muhammad III and played an important role in putting down a rebellion at Bidar in 1487, after which he requested a posting to Telangana. Over the course of Sultan Quli's almost 50-year tenure as tarafdar (governor, or holder of a province), Telangana evolved into an independent and prosperous kingdom, and Golconda became its shining capital.

The position of this emergent state was threatened, however, by Sultan Quli's own longevity. One of several eligible heirs waiting in the wings as the sultan reached his 80s, Sultan Quli's son **Jamshid** (r. 1543-50), impatient to take the throne, is alleged to have murdered his father, and then imprisoned, killed, or forced his other brothers to flee Golconda. One of these brothers, Ibrahim, was forced to take refuge at Vijayanagara, where he spent the next seven years.

After Jamshid's death of natural causes in 1550, his adolescent son Subhan (r. 1550) was chosen to succeed, but **Ibrahim** was summoned from Vijayanagara by those at Golconda who remained loyal to him. Ibrahim proceeded to Golconda, where he was warmly welcomed by the people of the city and proclaimed sultan. Upon his accession to the Qutb Shahi throne, the new ruler (r. 1550-80)

Golconda, inscribed cenotaph of Sultan Quli

became embroiled at once in the intrigues of the Deccan and the jockeying for power among the sovereigns of neighboring Bijapur, Bidar, Ahmadnagar, Berar and Vijayanagara. Though still grateful to Ramaraya of Vijayanagara, at whose court he had spent his exile, Ibrahim eventually joined an alliance with the three other major Deccani sultanates against Vijayanagara, resulting in the 1565 defeat of Vijayanagara and the death of Ramaraya. Upon this victory Golconda gained new territory and received large sums of money and jewels from the Vijayanagara treasuries, which financed an extensive building campaign at the fort.

Ibrahim Qutb Shah had neglected to appoint an heir before his death in 1580, and so it was left to his ministers to choose which of his six sons should succeed him. They eventually settled on the 14-year-old **Muhammad Quli** (r. 1580-1612). During his reign, the constant wars among the Deccan sultans, so typical of the early to mid-16th century, had quieted, and the Qutb Shahi economy continued to thrive, with diamond mining becoming an increasingly important source of revenue. The dynasty's largest mine was at Kulur to the southeast of Golconda, not far from the port of Masulipatnam (known colloquially as Machlipatnam). Here, during the long reign of Abdullah (r. 1626-72), was discovered the famous Koh-i Nur diamond, which originally weighed 756 carats, and now forms part of the British crown jewels.

Golconda,
Tomb of Ibrahim
Qutb Shah

Hyderabad, Char Kaman, entrance to the Qutb Shahi palace zone

The establishment of European trading firms in the Deccan created another source of income for the kingdom. Of the various East India Companies that were commissioned to conduct trade with India and East Asia on behalf of European states in the early 17th century, those from Holland, Denmark, England and Portugal each had a presence in the Deccan. The Qutb Shahi kingdom profited from their presence by collecting taxes on all exports and levying port charges; in addition, local goods found new markets throughout Southeast Asia and Europe. Golconda attained renown for two types of manufactures: printed and painted textiles that were a specialty of the kingdom's coastal zone (on the Bay of Bengal, particularly around Srikakulam, Masulipatnam and Pulicat); and steel products, especially swords, which were manufactured in the areas near mines (such as Indalwai, northwest of Golconda). Forests around the port of Masulipatnam also supplied a thriving ship-building business.

With all of this wealth streaming in, Muhammad Quli decided to establish a new capital city in the year 1000 of the Islamic calendar (equivalent to CE 1591). He named his city Hyderabad, although legend relates that it was also called Bhagnagar, in honour of Bhagmati, the sultan's favourite courtesan. More likely, Bhagnagar was a corruption of Baghnagar, City of Gardens. Hyderabad was located 8 kilometres east of Golconda, and was filled with monuments set in and amongst tree-lined streets. Unlike Golconda, which remained the fortified retreat for defending the kingdom, the new city was never walled and was planned primarily to impress its visitors with its luxury.

Because Muhammad Quli had no male heirs he selected **Muhammad**, a nephew, to be his successor, and married the boy to his daughter, Hayat Bakhshi Begum. As ruler (r. 1626-72), Muhammad's chief concern was the threat of Mughal invasion, which would become much more serious in the decades to come.

After the death of Muhammad, his oldest son **Abdullah** was proclaimed sultan. He was only 14 at the time and for the first years of his reign (r. 1626-72) his mother, the capable Hayat Bakhshi Begum, acted as his regent. In 1630, when the armies of the Mughal emperor Shah Jahan finally conquered the Ahmadnagar sultanate to the north, which had shielded Golconda from the Mughals, Abdullah was forced to sign a deed of submission to Shah Jahan. He was forced to have Friday prayers recited in the name of Shah Jahan, mint coins with the Mughal imprimatur, pay an annual tribute, and provide aid for the Mughals' further conquests in the south. Shah Jahan's son Aurangzeb was then named viceroy of the Deccan.

Portrait of Abu'l Hasan, last of the Qutb Shahis (Courtesy San Diego Museum of Art)

Abdullah had no sons, and eventually settled on **Abu'l Hasan**, (r. 1672-87) husband of his youngest daughter, to succeed him. This was an unusual choice given that Abu'l Hasan had little prior experience at the court and had chosen to reside as an ascetic at a *khanqah* (retreat for Sufis) just outside the city. His reign, which lasted 15 years, marks a difficult period in the history of the Qutb Shahi dynasty. This sultan allowed his ministers to run state affairs, and contemporary sources remark on the terrible condition of people in the countryside, impoverished as a result of rapacious government policies.

THE MUGHALS AND THE NIZAMS

Outside of the court, the Mughals and the Marathas, a group of warriors from the west coast of the Deccan, became a major concern. By the 1680s **Aurangzeb**, now Mughal emperor, had decided he must complete the annexation of the remaining two sultanates of the Deccan. He attacked and captured Golconda's neighbor Bijapur in 1686, and then surrounded Golconda in January of 1687. The siege lasted until September, when a traitor in the fort opened a gate on the eastern side and allowed the Mughals to slip in during the night. Aurangzeb himself entered triumphantly through the Fateh Darwaza (Victory Gate). Abu'l Hasan surrendered and was imprisoned at the Daulatabad fort, some 575 kilometres to the northwest. He died in captivity several years later and was buried at a Sufi shrine in nearby Khuldabad.

Meanwhile, Aurangzeb camped at Hyderabad while the treasuries of both Qutb Shahi cities were inventoried, packed, and sent to Delhi. By the time the emperor left the Deccan in 1688, a new governor named Jan Sipar Khan had taken up residence in Hyderabad.

Over the next few years, Mughal governors continued to be appointed to administer the Deccan. Of these, the most significant was Qamar al-Din Chin Qilich Khan, who in 1713 was given the titles of Asaf Jah and **Nizam ul-Mulk**, and placed in charge of all six Mughal provinces in the Deccan. His fortunes within the Mughal administration changed several times over the next few years, and by 1724 he had wearied of

Golconda, Fateh Darwaza, the gate through which Aurangzeb entered the city

intrigues at the Mughal capital. He decided instead
to make his future in the Deccan, left the Mughal
capital and moved down to the city of Aurangabad.
Working hard to consolidate power in lands where
he had hitherto had little experience, he in time
established independent rule over the entire Deccan.
His descendants, known as the Asaf Jahi dynasty,
remained in power until 1948.

Nizam ul-Mulk's first three successors, Nasir
Jung (r. 1748-50), Muzaffar Jung (r. 1750-51) and
Salabat Jung (r. 1751-62), struggled to maintain the
fledgling Asaf Jahi state as competing powers fought
for control of the region. The Marathas, as well as
commanders from the French and English East India
Companies, which now had colonial aims in India,
all sought the rich and prosperous domains of the
Nizams. These three Asaf Jahi rulers relied more
heavily on the French, who at this time provided
military support in the wars for succession and were
rewarded with the revenues of large estates within
the kingdom. Typically, however, they are not considered part of the Asaf
Jahi line and it is only their successor, **Nizam ʿAli Khan** (r. 1762-1803),
who is considered Asaf Jah II.

Portrait of
Nizam ʿAli Khan,
the 2nd Nizam
(Courtesy San
Diego Museum
of Art)

Nizam 'Ali Khan was able to maintain power for long enough to
provide some stability to the Hyderabad state. He also switched alliances
from the French to the British, and agreed to support them in their
campaign for territorial gains. This, most significantly, meant providing
aid during the four Mysore Wars that took place between 1767 and
1799, in the course of which the British defeated the rulers of the
powerful Mysore state to the Nizam's south.

These wars fully established the British as the premiere European
power in the Deccan, and signalled the end of French influence in the
region. After this time, it would no longer be possible for someone like
Michel Joachim Raymond, a charismatic French mercenary who came
to be known as Musa Rahim, to gain the confidence of the Nizam as a
military advisor. The power of the British in the subcontinent at large
had been growing since the initial treaties for trade between India
and England were signed in the early 1600s. Victories such as those in

Pavilion and obelisk of Raymond's Tomb

Bengal in 1757 shifted their role from that of trading partner to that of ruling power, and the East India Company continued to spread into other regions, using native rulers to govern, but installing **Residents**, or advisors, at their courts.

In 1779 such a Resident was appointed to Hyderabad, which had been named the Asaf Jahi capital in 1763. The acceptance of such advisors changed the course of the dynasty's fate; despite enormous wealth and resources, later Nizams were rather removed from the affairs of state and often out of touch with the rapidly changing political scene of the 19th and 20th centuries. By the early 1800s, the Nizams were required to support the Hyderabad Contingent, one of many other financial obligations to the British advisors, which in the British accounting left the Nizams perpetually in debt despite the enormous income the state generated each year. The Contingent was settled in a cantonment northeast of central Hyderabad, in an area named Secunderabad after the 3rd Nizam, **Sikander Jah** (r. 1803-29). During his reign the British also took over the right of appointing the *diwan*, or prime minister, to the Nizam.

Under the 4th Nizam, **Nasir al-Daula** (r. 1829-57), the important province of Berar in the northern part of the Deccan was ceded to the British as the debts owed to them continued to mount. This situation changed with the appointment of Salar Jung I, made minister at the young age of 24, who would go on to serve three Nizams between 1853 and 1883. Salar Jung instituted a number of reforms that helped ease the financial crisis; among other acts, he took a pay cut that allowed state workers below him to receive their salary on a regular basis – something that had not occurred for many years.

The reforms were slowed on the accession of the 5th Nizam, **Afzal al-Daula** (r. 1857-69) in part because of the events of the Indian Uprising, or Mutiny, of 1857. Supporters among the population of Hyderabad were quickly put down, and the Nizam and Salar Jung strongly expressed their allegiance to the British. Afterwards, the British colonial government, now under Crown Rule rather than that of the East India Company, assured Hyderabad immunity from annexation and cancelled a major debt in the Nizam's name, so that his fiscal standing improved even further.

Coming to the throne at age three, the 6th Nizam, **Mahbub 'Ali Khan** (r. 1869-1911) would become known as The Beloved, and is still remembered fondly in Hyderabad history. Though supposed to have spent vast sums on habits such as never wearing the same clothes twice, he is said to have had a common touch, slipping out into the city in disguise in order to observe his subjects. The noteworthy cultural events of his era are the replacement of Persian with Urdu as the state language, and the appointment of the renowned Raja Deen Dayal as court photographer in 1885. The major tragedy of his reign was the flood of 1908, which caused mass destruction to the city and loss among its population, which the Nizam attempted to ease with charitable donations.

Hyderabad, the
Residency

HYDERABAD, GOLCONDA

The 7th Nizam, **Mir Osman`Ali Khan** (r. 1911-48), was for a period of time reputedly the world's richest man, and his state was considered a model in the Muslim world. After his two sons married the daughter and niece of Abdul Majid II, the last Caliph of the Ottoman Empire of Turkey, he was also considered the savior of the supreme Islamic authority. Mir Osman`Ali Khan was a quirky figure, though. Though famously miserly, he did much for the people of his city, establishing a hospital, library and a university, and instituting the Hyderabad State Bank. In addition, he founded an archaeological department that undertook restoration work and carried out much important research.

Nonetheless, the 7th Nizam made a major misstep in the most significant political decision of his reign. He believed he could maintain a state independent of India and Pakistan, and refused to join either at the time of independence from Great Britain in 1947. A sovereign state in the middle of the new Republic of India was untenable, however. In 1948 Hyderabad was invaded by the Indian army; the Nizam and his commanders could offer little resistance and with much bloodshed the state was subsumed into India. Like the other princes throughout the country, Mir Osman`Ali Khan was allowed to maintain his titles and a privy purse, and when he died in 1967 his grandson Mukarram Jah was permitted to succeed him. He is still considered the current Nizam but the position is merely symbolic since all titles and perquisites were abolished in 1974. While the current Nizam himself has been little involved in Hyderabad since the 1970s, his family has recently done much in the way of historical preservation as well as maintaining hospitals, nursing colleges and schools.

CULTURE AND SOCIETY

The heritage of the Deccan represents a melding of many different cultural streams. The Qutb Shahi sultans had Persian origins, and strong ties to Iran remained a feature of courtly life until the end of the dynasty. Calligraphers, poets, artists, and ministers all moved to the region and were able to assimilate into the local court scene. Other populations from across the Islamic world also found their way to Hyderabad, as well as Europeans lured by trade prospects, and Africans, brought to India originally as slaves but able to rise to appointments as the advisors and protectors of the sultans. The result was the creation of a body of art,

literature, religious traditions and even cuisine that had a unique multi-ethnic flair that pervades Hyderabad's identity still today.

The earliest **paintings and illustrated manuscripts** from Golconda reflect the dynasty's origins in Iran, and the kind of training Indian artists received at the time, which was based on contemporary Iranian styles. This way of painting matched the nature of the texts being made for the Golconda patrons in the 1570s and 1580s, which were classical in content – among them such famous Persian language works as the *Khamsa* (*Quintet*) of the poet Nizami (d. 1209). During the course of the 17th century, other kinds of manuscripts – with poetry in Dakhni (the local version of Urdu), or albums combining samples of painting and calligraphy – became more popular, and unique forms of Golconda painting developed. Artists also started to experiment with the imagery and methods of depicting perspective and volume that they observed in the European paintings and engravings that were becoming available in the Deccan. By the 1650s, painting styles changed again and a strong Mughal influence can be seen in the paintings made for the sultan Abdullah and his courtiers.

Under the Nizams of the 18th century, local artists such as the portraitist Venkatchellam created paintings in a style that had developed from earlier modes. The 19th century brought greater changes. Just as European styles of architecture became popular, it was more common for the works of art and decorative objects adorning these spaces to be imported from abroad. In the 1840s, the invention of photography all but obviated the work of court artists – now cameras were used for formal portraits and to capture important events at the court. The Nizams were among the wave of rulers in India to hire photographers as permanent members of staff. In Hyderabad, Raja Deen Dayal, whose descendants still run a studio in Secunderabad, was the long-term royal photographer. He not only captured the personalities of the court, but was also sent on assignment to photograph the landscape and monuments of the Nizam's vast domains.

Throughout this period, the eastern coast of the sultanate was the centre of production for

Golconda, polo match, ca 1570 (Courtesy San Diego Museum of Art)

beautifully dyed and printed fabrics. Known as *kalamkaris*, these textiles were made through a multi-step process in which each color of a design was applied individually with the assistance of the appropriate resists and mordants, so that the cotton fabric went through at least eight treatments and the composition emerged only at the end when the final dye had been applied. These textiles were traded throughout Southeast Asia, the Far East and Europe. For each of these markets fabric in different formats was produced, and buyers remarked on the brightness and fastness of the hues, unmatched by contemporary dyeing techniques anywhere else in the world.

In the realm of **language and literature**, the Persian influence was initially the strongest. Through the Qutb Shahi and most of the Asaf Jahi periods, court affairs were conducted in Persian, and historical chronicles and works of literature were also composed in that language. Immigrants from Iran were welcomed at the court, and the Persian Nowruz (New Year) festival was celebrated annually in Hyderabad. In addition, the Qutb Shahi sultans maintained close diplomatic relations with the Safavids of Iran, both because of the Iranian shahs' Shi'a faith, but also because they had, together with the Safavids, a common enemy in the Sunni Mughals of northern India. Although the political connections were less relevant in the time of the Nizams, and Urdu

Hyderabad,
Badshahi
`Ashurkhana

gradually replaced Persian as the medium for the court affairs and education, ties to Persian culture remain strong in Hyderabad.

Dakhni was another language that grew out of the Islamic cultural sphere. It was born in northern India as Urdu, a version of Hindi written in the Persian alphabet and including many Persian and Arabic loan words. In the Deccan the language had its own evolution. Among the best known works in Dakhni are the verses of Muhammad Quli, including love poems in which he takes on a female persona, a genre unique to this language.

The introduction of Persian and Urdu into the Deccan was balanced by the continuing use of the local regional language of Telugu. Ibrahim Qutb Shah, for instance, was a patron of Telugu literature, commissioning works in that language from the leading poets of the age. The 16th century in fact witnessed a renaissance of Telugu literature, at which time poets recast Indian classics such as the *Mahabharata* and *Ramayana*. In so doing they imposed complicated linguistic challenges on themselves, using a pure form of Telugu that avoided Sanskrit loan words, or composing in the *niroshthya* style, in which no labial vowels or consonants could be used.

In terms of **religion**, the Qutb Shahi sultans were Shi'a Muslims and the Asaf Jahi Nizams were Sunnis, while the nobility were of both Muslim and Hindu faiths. The general population also included Muslims of both sects, but the largest proportion was Hindu. There is substantial evidence for the mixing of these groups even at the time of religious observances. One such occasion was Muharram, the first month of the Muslim calendar and a period of remembrance marking the death of the Prophet Muhammad's grandson Husain at the battle of Karbala in 680. Mourners meet in groups to recite dirges and gather in 'ashurkhanas, buildings where 'alams (metal standards) symbolizing those carried by Husain and his partisans, are displayed. In the Qutb Shahi period this event was observed on a large scale, and historical sources mention that Hindus in the villages surrounding the capital also observed Muharram. For this part of the population, dirges were composed in Telugu.

In time, a special procession called the Langar was added to the Muharram rituals. This rite is performed in thanksgiving for the safe return of Abdullah, who as a young prince had been carried off by a mad elephant. Abdullah was missing for several days but the elephant miraculously brought him back to the city on the first of Muharram.

Although the Asaf Jahis were Sunni, public observances of Muharram continued and the Langar procession was also still held. Today Muharram is a major feature of Hyderabad's religious calendar, and the *ashurkhanas* of the 16th and 17th century are still in use.

From the Hindu calendar, a number of **seasonal festivals** were adopted by the Qutb Shahi court. The Dakhni poems of Muhammad Quli mention, for instance, celebrations of Basant and Holi in the spring, and tell us that a garden in the area of the Naya Qil'a within Golconda was used particularly for these celebrations. These holidays remained important under the Asaf Jahis, whose Hindu minsters provided patronage for these events, and they continue to be celebrated today.

The **cuisine** of Hyderabad also reflects the city's mixture of traditions. Generally rich and meat-heavy (but delicious), the food is based on a foundation of Mughal cookery from northern India combined with techniques and flavors from Iran, Central Asia and the immediate region. Many dishes are infused with underlying sour tang by way of tamarind, lemon or yogurt; and a *baghar*, a mixture of chilies and spices cooked quickly in hot oil, is often added as the final touch. The local specialty is *biryani* (a meat and rice combination), typically served with *baghare baigan* (eggplant) and *mirchi ka salan* (green pepper curry). *Haleem*, made during Ramadan, is a paste of wheat and meat that is cooked for hours to reach the proper consistency.

Hyderabad, Langar Procession; photograph by Raja Deen Dayal ca 1897 (Courtesy Clark Worswick) *See also photo on pages 98-99*

Visiting the historical monuments of Hyderabad by location is the most practical way to tour the city, and so these are described here by urban sector rather than in chronological order. To give context for the individual buildings, however, a brief summary of the city's growth over time is provided.

GROWTH OF THE CITY

As already mentioned, Hyderabad was founded in the year 1000 of the Islamic calendar (CE 1591). Aside from the millennial associations of this choice, the city was established to mark the newfound status of the Qutb Shahi dynasty, much elevated since the selection of Golconda as their capital. The new city was also meant to solve some very practical problems. As Golconda flourished and its population grew through the course of the 16th century, the fort had become crowded, and there were complaints of unsanitary conditions. Ibrahim Qutb Shah first ordered the search for a location for a new capital, and seems to have settled on a site near the current location of Hyderabad, where he built a massive water reservoir, the Husainsagar, now called **Tank Bund**, and a bridge from the north to the south side of the Musi River, known as **Purana Pul** (Old Bridge). This site possessed various advantages: it was on a hospitable plain with a good supply of water and it was situated near the main road running between Golconda and Masulipatnam.

Ibrahim died in 1580, soon after the bridge and reservoir were completed and before he had time to develop this site further. His son Muhammad Quli would, however, utilize it for the new city of Hyderabad. Having decided to move from Golconda, Muhammad Quli asked his minister Mir Mumin Astrabadi, to create a plan for the

PAGES 30-31
Empress Gate leading to the Residency (engraving by William Miller after a watercolour of Captain Grindlay, 1830s)

BELOW
Purana Pul, or Old Bridge

HYDERABAD, GOLCONDA

new capital. In 1591 construction started with the monument known as **Charminar** (Four Towers), and a congregational mosque next to it, continuing with a plaza to the north, the **Char Kaman** (Four 'Bows' or Arches), to the west of which were extensive palaces and gardens. He also built a hospital, the **Dar al-Shifa**, and the **Badshahi Ashurkhana**, in which to hold observances during Muharram.

Much of Muhammad Quli's city was destroyed in the series of sieges suffered by Hyderabad in the late 17th century, when Golconda fell to the Mughals, and in the early 18th century, when it was besieged and sacked several times by the Marathas and roaming groups of bandits. On various occasions the Mughal governor had to move to better-fortified Golconda until finally, in the early 18th century, walls were also built to enclose Hyderabad. (These walls were mostly demolished in the 1950s to allow for expansion of the city.)

Charminar

The next major changes took place in the mid- to late 18th century when the city was occupied by the Asaf Jahi rulers, who had moved from Aurangabad and taken it as their capital. They built their palaces, such as the **Chowmahalla** and **Purani Haveli**, in the area around the 16th-century Charminar, and the heart of the city remained south of the river until the British Resident James Kirkpatrick (1798-1805) constructed a palatial mansion, the **Residency**, on the north side of the Musi. As additional British settlements developed even further to the north in Secunderabad and Bolarum, the focus of the city's activities shifted in that direction.

As a result, crossings over the Musi became more important to the functioning of the city, and it became necessary for the walled city, the base of the Nizams, to communicate more fluently with the districts around it. The Purana Pul was located well west of the city centre, and

Purani Haveli

so was supplemented by the 1831 Oliphant (now Chaderghat) Bridge that provided more direct access to the Residency, and the 1859 Afzal Bridge, also known as **Naya Pul** (New Bridge). This latter bridge aligning with the north-south road running from Charminar was particularly transformative; for the first time that route had a natural passage over the river rather than simply terminating at it. This street became an impressive processional route straight from the Nizam's residence at Chowmahalla, through the city's landmark 16th-century monuments, and across the river to the Residency or the Nizam's country retreats in the north. A new gate, the Afzal Darwaza was built 1861 (but demolished 1954), which opened in the city walls at the point where the road from inside the city met the bridge, and a new mosque, the Afzal Ganj Mosque, was built nearby. The architecture of this period initially drew from Qutb Shahi traditions but the popularity of the Neo-Classical European style, first introduced at the Residency, became the norm for the palaces of the richest aristocrats by the end of the 19th century.

The devastating flood of 1908 was another milestone in the planning and development of the city. In the middle of an unprecedented rainstorm, dams outside the city broke and the Musi rose over its banks, killing approximately 15,000 people and ruining 19,000 homes. This tragedy prompted the Nizam's administration

King Koti Palace

to reassess the city's plan and a survey was commissioned from the engineer Mokshagundam Visvesvaraya. As a result of his findings, a series of new **Dams and Dykes** were constructed to control the amount of water entering the city through the river, and the most congested neighborhoods closest to the river were razed, to be eventually replaced by several public institutions.

Changing architectural course yet again, these monuments were built in a style that combined elements of the Gothic Revival popular in England with the earlier Qutb Shahi and Mughal traditions. Another major change was the fact that the 7[th]Nizam himself shifted his residence north of the river to **King Koti Palace**, which he occupied in 1914. Such a move northwards had been resisted for over a century, but in transferring to the more British side of the Musi, the Nizam constructed a court building, a library, a hospital and a college on the banks of the river so that the area was quite visibly linked to him. Today, the Old City around Charminar is one of the more insular neighborhoods in the city, having lost its role as the seat of power.

The city's spread north has continued in the period since the 1950s, after Hyderabad joined the Republic of India, and the city was named the capital of the state of Andhra Pradesh (now temporarily of both Telangana and Andhra Pradesh). Neighborhoods such as

Begumpet and Secunderabad, north of Tank Bund, now lie well within the urban limits of the city. To the west, Banjara Hills, once on the furthest edges of city and barely inhabited, is fully developed, and its characteristic granite outcrops are being blasted apart to allow for more construction. Further west are the latest suburbs in Jubilee Hills, and beyond is **Hi-Tec City** (Hyderabad Information Technology and Engineering Consultancy City), the newest addition to Hyderabad. Its ultra-modern glass-sheathed buildings, housing the Indian headquarters of some of the world's top information technology companies, signal the new direction of architecture in Hyderabad.

THE OLD CITY

See photo on page 33

Hyderabad's Old City is the area centred on the early monuments built at the site under the Qutb Shahis. While the modern metropolis has developed for the most part north of the Musi, the heart of the city was originally located to the south and was based around the **Charminar**, the first building erected in Hyderabad when founded by Muhammad Quli. This is unusual structure is located at the crossing of two major roads, one running north to the river and south to an area of garden estates including the Koh-i Tur, a hill where the 19th-century Falaknuma Palace now stands, and the other running west to Golconda and east to Masulipatnam.

The Charminar is a four-sided monument opened up with tall arches on each face and with a slender circular *minar*, or tower, at each corner. Around the first storey runs a gallery overlooking the interior of the building (at the level where a clock is now affixed), and above that is a mosque; these are reached by stairs in each *minar*. The architectural decoration typical of other Qutb Shahi monuments is also found here – carved stucco detailing abounds in the decorative medallions in the spandrels of each arch and under the eaves and brackets of each storey. The rings of petal-like projection at each level of the *minar*s and supporting the small domes are also typical of the buildings at Golconda. But how the structure functioned is something of a mystery, and the placement of a mosque at the top of such a structure is unusual. It remains unclear who would have had access to it and how often it was used.

The first floor gallery is open to visitors (ticket required), and affords magnificent views across the Old City as well as opportunities to inspect interior stucco details, such as the decorative calligraphic *'alam*s.

Charminar,
upper mosque

Special permission is required to enter the mosque above. It has a prayer hall of five bays topped by shallow domes, and porticoes on the three other sides of the small courtyard in front of it. The stuccowork here is delicate and well-preserved, but little of it is original, for the Charminar has been repaired at various times since its construction: the west minaret was struck by lightning; the stucco work refurbished in 1824; and the clocks added in 1889.

Extending west from Charminar is the **Lad Bazaar**, a shopping area believed to date to the Qutb Shahi era. The current buildings were erected in the late 18th century, and today the area is noted for its stalls selling bangles and wedding paraphernalia.

To the north of the Charminar was a spacious plaza, approximately 260 metres square, with a large octagonal pool in the middle. In the middle of each of the four sides of the plaza was a tall arch, known collectively as **Char Kaman**, dating from 1592. On the west side of

See photo on page 16

HYDERABAD

the plaza were the **Qutb Shahi Palaces**, which extended as far north as the Musi. The plaza acted as a forecourt for those waiting to see the sultan, who was concealed behind a spike-studded sandalwood gate protected by royal elephants and African guards. More guards were posted inside the eastern arch on the opposite side of the plaza, and drums sounded from here to mark the passage of the day, and to note the entrance or exit of the sultan.

The Qutb Shahi palaces do not survive, but visitors such as Jean de Thèvenot, a French jewel merchant who visited Golconda in the 17th century, mention the names of several of the buildings, and describe the multi-storyed constructions and the beautiful trees and plants around them. The poetry of Muhammad Quli, written in Dakhni, also names his palaces and rhapsodizes about the exploits (amorous and otherwise) that took place within them. From these various written sources we learn that there was a southern enclosure with the Privy Council Chamber, and a northern enclosure with the royal wardrobe house and other royal offices. Other palaces included the Chandan Mahal (Sandalwood Palace), Gagan Mahal (Heavenly Palace) and Sajan Mahal.

The arch on the south side of the plaza provided access to the city's **Jami Masjid**, which was constructed between the Char Kaman and the Charminar. This building is nearly lost today among the shops that encroach on all sides and by the concrete extension built in front of the prayer hall. Even so, visitors can see a part of the original structure once they locate its whitewashed minarets behind the stores and navigate down an alley to its entrance. The prayer hall is preceded by a walled

Jami Masjid,
mihrab

Mecca Masjid

HYDERABAD, GOLCONDA

HYDERABAD

Mecca Masjid,
graves of the
Asaf Jahi family

courtyard with a gate, and there was a madrasa and baths as part of
the complex. An inscription once affixed above the gate praised Sultan
Muhammad Quli and provided 1597 as the date of construction. Quite
small for a congregational mosque, the prayer hall is just five aisles wide
and one bay deep. The inscription around the *mihrab* (prayer niche) is
taken from Chapter 2, Verses 137-8 of the Qur'an, and is signed by its
calligrapher, Jamal al-Din Husain. The building was repaired extensively
in the early 19th century by the order of Nizam `Ali Khan.

Much more impressive and fitting of the new capital is
the grandly scaled mosque built by Muhammad Quli's successor
Muhammad. Construction of the **Mecca Masjid**, southwest of the
Charminar, started in 1617. Work at the site continued for decades,

Chowmohalla
Palace, Khilwat

although the prayer hall has a facade of simply dressed stone, and
the massive minarets, which only rise one storey, remain unfinished.
The stunted domes that now cap them were added by Aurangzeb,
along with the main gateway into the courtyard, after his capture of
Hyderabad in 1687. The mosque's name is also attributed to this period,
when the legend emerged that bricks above the central arch of the
prayer hall had been fashioned from earth brought from Mecca. Inside
the prayer hall are 15 bays that are 25 metres tall and are graced with
enormous chandeliers.

In the spacious courtyard in front of the mosque are the graves
of 16 members of the Asaf Jahi family (later covered by a pavilion).
Those buried here include Nizam`Ali Khan (d. 1803), Sikander Jah

Chowmahalla Palace, Khilwat interior

(d. 1829), Nasir al-Daula (d. 1857), Afzal al-Daula (d. 1869) and Mahbub `Ali Khan (d. 1911).

South of the Mecca Masjid is the **Chowmahalla Palace** (Four Halls Palace). The complex was begun in 1750 by Salabat Jung, but the Nizams' primary residence shifted to the Purani Haveli in the early 19th century before Chowmahalla was reoccupied by Nasir al-Daula, and completely renovated in the time of Afzal al-Daula. The palaces originally spread over 18 hectares; today a core of 4 hectares has been restored and can be visited.

On entering through a modest gate, visitors face a long rectangular water tank lined with colonnades, now housing a souvenir shop, canteen, and a photo studio in which they can don period costumes and pose for sepia-toned pictures. There are also halls with displays of costume and photographs from the royal collections. The famous Darbar Hall (ca 1780), or Khilwat, is opposite. Painstakingly restored, it boasts a marble throne platform and floors, as well as chandeliers of Belgian crystal. Mukarram Jah was installed here as the 8th Nizam in 1967.

Beyond this is another courtyard on each side of which is a palace hall, the ensemble that gives the complex its name. On the east side is the Mihtab Mahal (Sun Palace), featuring lobed arches that spring from double baluster columns of a style prevalent in the Mughal era. The Aftab Mahal (Moon Palace) on the west, in contrast, has Ionic columns and Neo-Classical mouldings. The Afzal Mahal on the south is again in a Neo-Classical style, but with Corinthian columns. The Tahniat Mahal on the north is its mirror. These are all the work of the Afzal al-Daula who made a set of improvements to the palace when also constructing his bridge, city gate and mosque. Other buildings surround the two main courtyards, representing the type of structure that must have originally dotted the vast compound. In them are displayed clocks, vintage cars and other collections of the Nizams.

Princess Esra, former wife of Mukarram Jah, has spearheaded the massive conservation project that has rehabilitated the buildings of the Chowmahalla, and preserved its assemblages of royal clothing, arms and photographs. Some of these were stored in rooms locked after the death of the 7th Nizam in 1967, and only opened in 2001 when Princess Esra's renovation efforts began.

Further south of this area are two sites related to the aristocratic Paigah family, second only to the Asaf Jahis in the Hyderabad hierarchy and in wealth. Several male members of the family served as advisors to Nizams, and the women of the families intermarried. The **Paigah Cemetery** was founded in the 1790s and located close to the Dargah of Barhanah Shah (d. 1686), a Sufi saint from Iraq. In 1983 the family turned over care of the cemetery to the State Archaeology Department, which now maintains the site.

See photos on pages 4, 5 and 6-7

The Paigah Cemetery is entered through a formal gateway, and contains several pavilions and a mosque on the western side, opposite a water tank. The style of the monuments is a Mughalized version of Qutb Shahi architecture, with baluster columns and cusped arches decorated with carved stucco flourishes. One marked difference from Qutb Shahi precedents, however, is the use of ornamental stucco pineapples along the rooflines of the pavilions. This fruit was evidently an emblem of the family; sadly, only a few remain. The tombs are located within and around several white pavilions with extraordinary *jalis* (pierced stone screens). Many marble tombstones here are inlaid with colourful semi-precious stones.

Falaknuma (now Falaknuma Palace Hotel)

The **Falaknuma Palace** (The Heaven-Like, or Sky-Reflecting Palace) was built on a hilltop south of the city where Qutb Shahi sultans had also once retreated from the bustle of the capital. Its patron was Sir Viqar al-Umara, member of the Paigah family, and brother-in-law and prime minister of Mahbub`Ali Khan. Construction began in 1884 and lasted for nine years. In 1897 the 6th Nizam purchased the palace and it remained in the hands of the Nizam's Trust until 2000 when the Taj Hotel Group leased the building, opening it in 2010 as the luxurious Falaknuma Palace Hotel.

Filled with furnishings and textiles imported from England and France, the design for the palace was inspired by Sir Viqar's travels through Europe in 1882. The heavily Europeanized elements of the Falaknuma signalled a new trend in Hyderabadi architecture, one that diverged radically from the 18th- to mid-19th-century traditions, marking a change from the Chowmahalla, the more traditional palace that had served the Nizams and their families for decades. However, the Falaknuma did include women's quarters at the back, which conformed to earlier traditions.

Visitors to Falaknuma are now limited to those staying or dining at the hotel. If just coming for tea or dinner, one can see the Roman-styled entry hall (with an Italian marble fountain and a remarkable

Falaknuma,
fountain lobby

PAGES 48-49
Badshahi
`Ashurkhana,
interior

painted ceiling showing an eagle flying through the skies), and a wood-panelled study (with a unique coffered ceiling, beautifully restored and presented with original furnishings). Passing through the courtyard, now lined with bedroom suites, visitors may proceed to the Gol Bungalow, a balcony with cast-iron railings and a stained-glass dome, offering panoramic views over the landscape to the rear of the palace. Hotel guests can ascend the grand staircase lined with Italian marble statues of the Muses of ancient Greek mythology, as well as formal portraits of Sir Viqar and the 6th Nizam. From here they may roam through the ballroom, the ladies' sitting room, the men's games room complete with billiard table, and the banquet hall illuminated by great chandeliers and housing an amazingly long table seating more than 80 guests.

AROUND THE MUSI RIVER

North of the Charminar area, close to the Musi, are other monuments built at the time of Hyderabad's foundation, as well as the facilities added by the 7th Nizam, Mir Osman `Ali Khan.

The first group is located on the south side of the river. As it stands today the **Badshahi `Ashurkhana** preserves several phases of construction, but inscriptions date the first part of the building to 1592-96 and attribute it to the patronage of Muhammad Quli Qutb Shah. The

See photo on page 27

HYDERABAD

brilliantly coloured tile decoration was completed under Abdullah Qutb Shah in 1611, and the outer halls and wooden colonnades, as well as the entry gate, were added by Nizam`Ali Khan in about 1764.

As an 'ashurkhana, the building comes in use during Muharram, the Shi'a month of mourning. During that month 'alams are set up in the building, which is structured as a pavilion with walls on three sides enclosing a platform where the 'alams are displayed. Behind the platform the central niche functions as a mihrab, indicating the direction of Mecca, and it is filled with a hexagonal tile pattern. The niches on either side of the mihrab of the inner hall have hexagonal tile replicas of 'alams and the cloths that shield the poles that hold them. As no other Qutb Shahi building has such extensive tiling (at least not that survives), what we find here is the only clue to what must

Badshahi `Ashurkhana, tile panel

PAGES 48-49
Badshahi `Ashurkhana

have been a well-developed ornamental tradition. Visitors should note, however, that some of the decoration is painted, a restoration of areas of tile that have been lost.

The **Dar al-Shifa** (Place of Healing) was finished in 1595, and functioned as a medical school and teaching hospital specializing in Yunani (Greek) medicine. Its location near the Musi was chosen specifically for the healing winds coming off the river, and next to the building was a garden where herbs and plants with curative properties were grown. To add to the efficacy of the treatments administered by its doctors, was a relic enshrined in the building associated with Husain's son Zain al-Abidin, who had fallen ill at the battle of Karbala, and which

Dar al-Shifa,
entrance gate

was thought to confer blessings on the sick. This relic is now housed in a small *'ashurkhana* in the middle of the courtyard, which is visited during Muharram. The square structure is made up of four double-storey halls around a central courtyard. There are remains of the original stucco decoration, including representations of *'alams* balanced on the apexes of the arches.

The **Purani Haveli** (Old Palace) was constructed in 1777 for Sikander Jah by his father, Nizam`Ali Khan, on the site of a 16th-century estate. Occupied by Sikander initially, he and subsequent rulers then chose to live at the Chowmahalla Palace, until the 6th Nizam made it his primary residence. Long halls are situated around the sides of two adjacent courtyards. The architecture of the Purani Haveli is like that of the other late 19th-century palaces, drawing on European Neo-Classical engaged pilasters supporting pediments, and cornices with egg-and-dart molding. Since 2000 the building has housed the City Museum, and adjacent compounds for the women of the court, once connected to the main palace by subterranean tunnels, are now home to the Princess Esin Women's Educational Centre (established 1973).

See photos on pages 25 and 34

The museum documents the history of the city from the prehistoric settlements on the site to the present. Also on view are relics of the last two Nizams: visitors can walk through the almost 60-metre long wardrobe of Mahbub`Ali Khan, who is reputed to have given away his clothing after one wearing, and view exhibits from the reign of

Purani Haveli, walk-through wardrobe

Mir Osman 'Ali Khan, especially the throne used and gifts received on the occasion of his Silver Jubilee, which was celebrated in 1937.

In 1914 the 7th Nizam established a City Improvement Board to create a master plan for Hyderabad, and invited Vincent J. Esch to design several new monuments for him. Esch had come to India from England in 1898, soon after completing his architectural studies, and worked at Calcutta before agreeing to move to Hyderabad. His first building was the Kachiguda Railway Station located east of the city (described below), and the next three buildings were near each other facing the Musi River. The **High Court** (1916) is made of pink granite, quarried locally, combined with the red sandstone and white marble associated with Mughal buildings. The domes, now painted pink, were originally covered in blue tiles. The building draws heavily from Mughal models, and thus is quite different from the European-style architecture that had prevailed in Hyderabad at the turn of the 20th century.

Esch's next project was the **City High School for Boys** (now City College, 1917-20). It stands on a lower level of granite, roughly dressed; the façade rising from there is smooth plaster over stone. Though also derived in many ways from a Mughal architectural vocabulary, Esch himself described the building somewhat whimsically as 'Perpendicular Mogul Saracenic', indicating a whiff of Gothic influence. It is difficult to see the front of the building since the compound wall is so close, but a walk around it gives visitors a better sense of the building's original impression. It is laid out with triple-story arched openings in the middle of each side, long rows of verandahs with nicely detailed columns and capitals, and *chhatris* (domed kiosks) lining the parapet. Inside, many of the classrooms are still in their original condition.

One of the 7th Nizam's benefactions, the **Azah Khanah-i Zahra**, is an 'ashurkhana built in honor of his mother, Zahra Begum (d. 1941). It was designed by the engineer-architect Zain Yar Jang and the exterior relates to the Esch buildings nearby, combining clean lines with Indo-Islamic architectural flourishes. (The Indo-Saracenic style, that became popular in India in the second half of the 19th century, derived from

ABOVE
Azah Khanah-i
Zahra

TOP
High Court

Salar Jung
Museum

*See photo on
page 20*

Mughal and Deccani architecture and including *chhatris*, eaves with brackets, pierced screens and domes.) Inside, mourners gather during Muharram in a large, open hall oriented towards a platform where *'alam*s are displayed. The interior seems to draw from a western Islamic tradition, as seen in Cairene architecture, with columns topped by *muqarnas* (stalactite-like) capitals, and *muqarnas* in the dome above the *'alam*s. The second story gallery, protected by pierced screens, is reserved for women.

The **Salar Jung Museum**, Hyderabad's premiere art museum (closed Fridays), is based entirely on the collections of one remarkable man, Mir Yusuf 'Ali Khan, Salar Jung III (1889-1949). Refocusing his energies after being dismissed from official duties in 1914, Salar Jung collected thousands of works or art. Inspired by his grandfather's and father's acquisitions from their tours through Europe, Salar Jung assembled masterpieces of Islamic art to Pharonic Egyptian artefacts and European sculpture, paintings and decorative objects. After his death a museum was made out of these collections in his ancestral home, the Diwan Deori (since demolished); they are now housed in a purpose-built building inaugurated in 1968. The displays that are particularly popular with the public today are the marble 'Veiled Rebecca' (1876) from Italy, and a musical clock from England with figures that chime the hour. The real treasures of the museum, however, are the illustrated manuscripts, including many important Deccani works, the Qur'ans, and the Mughal jades.

Still on the south side of the river but further east is **Raymond's Tomb**, an obelisk and pavilion set on a hill with sweeping views marking the burial place of Michel Joachim Raymond (1755-98), French military advisor to Nizam`Ali Khan. Raymond arrived in Hyderabad in the 1780s and took over responsibility for casting cannons and making muskets; the Gun Foundry neighborhood in the city marks the location of his workshop. For a time he was also one the most valued supporters and advisors to the Nizam, and was accordingly granted a sizeable estate with significant revenues. Among the early group of Europeans at the Hyderabad court, Raymond assimilated into the local culture and

adopted many Indian habits. He remained a beloved figure and for a long time the anniversary of his death was observed. The stark simplicity of his funereal monument is often noted; the only decoration is an inscribed plaque on the obelisk with the initials "JR". The tomb has recently been rebuilt.

North of the river, just opposite the High Court and the Salar Jung Museum, are the hospital and library established by the 7th Nizam, and named after him as the **Osmania Hospital** (1925). Here Vincent Esch continued his work from the City High School in the 'Perpendicular Mogul Saracenic' style. At the time, it was among the best hospitals in the world, and certainly one of the largest. A sense of the scale on which the building was planned is immediate upon entry into an atrium several storeys tall and topped by a dome. From this extend wards more than 30 metres long and 8 metres wide. The formal garden in front of the building is now somewhat overgrown, obscuring the facade of the still-functioning hospital.

After Esch left Hyderabad in the mid-1920s, the public monuments of Mir Osman `Ali Khan were designed by employees of the Public Works Department. This office was responsible for all of the buildings in the Public Gardens and for the Asafiya Library (1929-34), now the **State Central Library**. A wide set of stairs leads up to a

grand arch providing entrance to the building; oddly, the brackets usually found under the eaves of buildings have been applied to this arch. Other elements of the exterior design follow the logic of Indo-Islamic architecture more closely, with typical pointed arches and pierced screen railings filling out the rest of the facade. The building is currently under renovation and the interior difficult to access. However, the entry hall is impressive, and some of the reading rooms upstairs reveal stuccowork seemingly based on models of Spanish Islamic architecture.

The Residency, interior staircase

See also photo on pages 22-23

Further north is the **Residency**. A British Resident was installed at Hyderabad in 1779; eventually this officer would report directly to the Governor-General in Calcutta. Residents at Hyderabad initially lived in a bungalow in a former royal garden, but James Achilles Kirkpatrick commissioned a much more impressive structure, built between 1803 and 1806. Reflecting well the contemporary political situation, the Nizam of Hyderabad was expected to fund the construction and furnishings of the building. The British Residency and its inhabitants have been recently immortalized in William Dalrymple's book *White Mughals* (2002). Although the building is now used by the Osmania Women's College, visitors may enter by requesting permission from the college president's office.

The Residency is the work of architect Samuel Russell, and its design is said to refer to the recently completed Government House in Calcutta; Kirkpatrick's aspirations were lofty indeed. The north side of the building, from which visitors today also approach, was oriented to the new British settlements in this part of the city. It presents a Neo-Classical façade — wide stairs, protected by a pair of lions, lead up to tall Corinthian columns headed by a pediment framing the seated lion and unicorn, the coat-of-arms of the East India Company. But the building's relationship to the Musi was also important. Although hard to see now due to the development of the surrounding neighborhood, the building is quite close to the river and because the city's main population centre was in fact south of the river, that route of access was commonly used at the time. The impressive Empress Gate standing in the garden offered entry from that side, and in 1831, an additional bridge across the Musi, closer to the Residency than the pre-existing ones, was built to ease access. Inside, a darbar hall (audience hall) 30 metres in length once hosted public functions. A gracefully curving double staircase with an elegant cast-iron balustrade leads to an upper balcony.

See engraving on pages 30-31

Behind the darbar hall of the Residency were kitchens and other buildings for the household staff, as well as a few remains of Kirkpatrick's marriage to the noblewoman Khairunnissa, with whom he had two children. The womens' quarters where Khairunnissa lived were torn down in 1860 by the then Resident George Yule, but visitors will still find a decaying plaster model of the Residency that Kirkpatrick had made for Khairunnissa, who would not leave the womens' quarters to see the main residence. Adjacent is a small cemetery. By 1826 the administrative tasks of the Resident's office had moved north, to an area near Secunderabad, and between the 1840s and 1860s the building was largely abandoned.

The **Kachiguda Railway Station** was designed by Vincent Esch in 1914. He had earlier experimented with the use of concrete in his buildings in Calcutta and continued those trials in Hyderabad, fashioning this structure, for example, completely out of pre-cast concrete. Although its method of construction was ultra-modern, the building was completed in an Indo-Saracenic style.

Kachiguda
Railway Station

TANK BUND SOUTH

The reservoir known today as **Tank Bund**, almost 18 kilometres in circumference, was originally called Husainsagar for the minister, Husain Shah Wali, who had it constructed in 1562 during the reign of Ibrahim Qutb Shah. The reservoir takes advantage of a natural depression in the ground in this area; alongside it an earthen embankment approximately one-kilometre long was constructed in order to collect rain and run-off water from the surrounding higher ground. The colossal monolithic statue of the Buddha in the middle of the lake was commissioned in the 1980s by the then Andhra Pradesh Chief Minister N.T. Rama Rao. It was finally erected on its base in 1992 after sinking into the reservoir two years earlier in the first installation attempt. A tomb in a revival Qutb Shahi style stands on the northeastern corner of the tank. It is dedicated to Sayedani Maa, mother of Nawab Abdul Haq Diler Jung, who died in 1883.

Tank Bund, with modern Buddha statue

Just south of Tank Bund, off of Nampally Circle, are the **Public Gardens** established in 1846 and embellished with several buildings under the last two Nizams. Directly inside the entrance is the **Andhra Pradesh State Museum**. The collections of the museum range from a single Egyptian mummy to Hindu and Buddhist sculptures, replica paintings of the Ajanta murals, and Mughal, Rajput and Deccani miniatures. The museum also owns a group of paintings by the Pakistani painter Abdur Rahman Chugtai (1899-1975), and there is a separate gallery devoted to Jain religious sculpture.

Opposite the museum is the **State Legislative Assembly** (1905-22). The building was begun by the 6th Nizam, and was intended for the celebration of his Silver Jubilee. His death preceded the completion of the building and it was repurposed as a Town Hall. The main block of the building is two storeys high, with the cusped arches, baluster columns and eaves resting on brackets of historical Indian buildings. The domed tower that rises two further storeys above that, however, represents a borrowing from European models. Special permission is required to enter the building.

Set in the gardens along with other small museums is **Jubilee Hall** (1936), marking the Silver Jubilee of the 7th Nizam. Like the Legislative Assembly and the Public Library, it was built by the Public Works Department after Vincent Esch had introduced elements of Indo-Islamic architecture back into Hyderabad's buildings.

Andhra Pradesh State Museum

Representing the second phase of building at Hyderabad, under Muhammad Qutb Shah, is the **Khairatabad Mosque** built in 1612 by the sultan's daughter for her tutor Mullah Abd al-Malik. The fine stuccowork on the facade of this small mosque is obscured by an addition to the building, but inside there is much to be admired, albeit under coats of green and gold paint. Especially noteworthy is the fine calligraphic design in the *mihrab*.

In 1836, the 4th Nizam Nasir al-Daula granted permission for the British Resident to construct a church in Hyderabad, the first permitted in Hyderabad proper. The designated plot was northwest of the Residency in an area known today as **Abids**. By 1844 St George's Church, a small building that is now the St George's Boys School, was complete. Two decades later the funds for a new building were raised by subscription, and donors included the Nizam and the staff of the

LEFT
St George's
Church

BELOW
Osmania
University

HYDERABAD, GOLCONDA

Residency. The wife of the resident George Yule laid the foundation stone in 1865; construction took a further 18 months.

The new **St George's Church** was designed by George William Marrett, Chief Engineer to the Nizam, and possibly architect of Falaknuma Palace. Its interior and exterior are decorated in a spare Neo-Gothic style with pointed arches, and a stained-glass window depicting the ascension of Christ.

King Koti Palace (now District Hospital King Koti) is a palace complex built by the noble Muhammad Kamal Khan, and when purchased by the 7th Nizam the residence was renamed King Koti to accommodate Kamal Khan's initials "KK" found all over the building. King Koti became the Nizam's primary residence from 1914 on. The complex had three parts: Nazri Bagh on the west, with the main residential buildings, still part of the Nizam's private estate; King Koti on the east, for official and ceremonial functions, now a hospital; and Osman Mansion in the center, demolished in the 1980s to make way for a new wing to the hospital. The 7th Nizam died in Osman Mansion but unlike his predecessors who were buried at the Mecca Masjid, he was laid to rest in a cemetery close to this palace. A pavilion with pierced screens encloses his grave, as well as those of his mother and wife.

See photo on page 35

About 5 kilometres east of this area is **Osmania University** (founded 1918; building inaugurated 1938), another of Mir Osman `Ali Khan's civic foundations. The main Arts College was built after the group of institutions designed by Vincent Esch for the 7th Nizam, and like those it fuses decorative elements from the vocabulary of Islamic architecture to the basic structure of a European facility. In this case, the Belgian architect Ernest Jaspar (1876-1940) took his direct inspiration from Egypt where he had previously worked. The building's entrance portal is based on that of the 14th-century Tomb of Sultan Hasan in Cairo, with a *muqarnas*, or honeycomb-like structure, in the vaulting. The pointed arches on slender columns of the second storey gallery of the facade are also reminiscent of architecture from the western Islamic world, but the columns of the first floor gallery seem more like those found in medieval Indian temples. Also part of the initial construction at the campus is the University Library. The university is distinguished as the first in India to have a native language as its medium, classes were taught in Urdu until 1948.

TANK BUND NORTH

After Sir Viqar al-Umara vacated the Falaknuma Palace, he moved back briefly to the family's residence in the city, the Deori Iqbal al-Daula in Shah Ganj, of which little survives, while construction of the new **Paigah Palace** was completed. He moved into this new residence in 1898. Like the Falaknuma this palace takes inspiration from European sources, though on a much reduced scale. The building now houses the U.S. Consulate General and cannot be visited without permission. The so-called **Spanish Mosque** to the north, on the Begumpet main road, was once a part of the palace compound and is loosely based on the Islamic architecture of southern Spain.

Vincent Esch also designed the **Hyderabad Public School** (1924). It was originally established as the Jagirdars College for sons of the city's land-owning families, and was envisioned along the lines of the English public school of Eton. Here Esch further carried out his experimentation with the Indo-Saracenic style, borrowing domes and pointed arches from Indian Islamic architecture.

Spanish Mosque

On the west side of Tank Bund is **Iram Manzil** (now Erramanzil), the Office of the Engineer-in-Chief, Roads and Buildings Department, but originally the palace of Nawab Fakhar ul-Mulk (1860-1934), a noble of the Salar Jung family and contemporary of Sir Viqar al-Umara. This palace is another example of the late 19th-century trend towards European-style grandeur, and the remaining residential block was once but a single element in a 160-hectare compound with formal gardens, tennis courts and polo grounds. Happily, much of the original decoration of the building can be glimpsed inside the offices that now occupy the building, hidden behind desks and files and under several coats of paint. Some rooms upstairs also show the intermingling of Mughal traditions within the overall European palatial design; carved stucco flourishes ornament cusped arches that rest on flaring baluster columns.

Iram Manzil

SECUNDERABAD

An alliance between Nizam ʿAli Khan and the British signed in 1798 included the proviso that British troops would be supplied to protect Hyderabad (although at the expense of the Nizam). A few years later a cantonment area for these troops was established in the far northeast corner of the city, readied in 1806 and named Secunderabad after the reigning Nizam, Sikander Jah. It would become the largest cantonment in India, housing 50,000 people in an area of more than 40 square kilometres, and laid out with a high street, called James Street, a parade ground and a racecourse. The area also had its own railway station and hospitals, and it was in Secunderabad that Sir Ronald Ross carried out

St John's Church, interior

the experiments that led to the identification of mosquitoes as the carriers of malaria. In 1860, the British Resident built a new Residency (replacing the one near the Musi) further north of Secunderabad, in the area known as Bolarum. This building is now called Rashtrapati Nilayam and is reserved for the use of the President of India.

St John's Church dates to 1813, and first served the forces of the Lancer's Line. A Baroque revival belfry was added in front of the Neo-Classical facade in 1923. Inside, the centre aisle is paved with Minton tiles from Staffordshire, England, now covered by carpet. Rattan pews stand under a teak ceiling, supported by Neo-Classical rounded arches and Doric columns.

The **Secunderabad Club** is only open to members and their guests, but shows the more genteel side of life in the cantonment. It was established in April 1878 and after several name changes became known as the Secunderabad Club in 1903. The original building at the site once belonged to Salar Jung I who stayed there on visits to the Viceroy or Resident. It is rustic in style, with stone walls and gabled, tiled roofs. Inside, the Men's Colonnade still has its colonial-era furniture and regimental shields. The addition to the north has further public rooms with Art Nouveau frescoes.

Secunderabad
Club

Trimulgherry, approximately 4.5 kilometers north of
Secunderabad, was an entrenched military camp surrounded by a stone
ditch. **All Saints Church** (1860) is Gothic in style with a long nave,
stained glass windows and a tower belfry. The **Military Prison**, built in
the 1858, has a castellated watchtower that overlooks four wings with
75 individual holding cells built in the Neo-Gothic style.

Some 6.5 kilometres northeast of the Secunderabad area
is the **Shrine of Maula `Ali**, built in commemoration of an event that
occurred in the 16th century. One night a courtier of Ibrahim Qutb Shah
had a vision of `Ali, son-in-law of the Prophet and a revered figure in the
Shi'a tradition. In his dream `Ali was seated on a hill with his right hand
resting on a rock. In the morning the courtier travelled from Golconda
and found the hill where indeed, a handprint had been impressed on the
rock. He immediately built a shrine over this rock and the anniversary
of his vision was celebrated during the Qutb Shahi period. The custom
was revived in the 1780s under Nizam `Ali Khan, despite his own Sunni
beliefs, and the anniversary evolved into a long festival starting on 13
Rajab, `Ali's birthday, and ending on 7 Rajab, the day of the vision. It
seems that the festival was a time in which social norms relaxed, and
the main sponsors of the festivities, hosting gatherings and handing out

food to the poor, were the city's wealthy courtesans. Climbing up the steps in the gigantic rock formation on which the shrine sits, visitors will pass several pavilions and a 17th-century Qutb Shahi mosque, and then go through a series of whitewashed gates. The shrine itself is of the Asaf Jahi period, while the mirrorwork inside is of even more recent vintage.

Nearby is the **Tomb of Mah Laqa Bai Chanda**, a famed 18th-century poetess and courtesan. The compound in which it stands was originally constructed as a place for musical gatherings and late-night poetry recitals during the annual festivals at Maula 'Ali, but she added a tomb when her mother died in 1792, and was herself was buried there in 1824. The decoration of the *baradari* (garden pavilion), mosque and tomb – comprising baluster columns, cusped arches and projecting porches covered by *bangla* roofs (curving, as in the style of buildings in Bengal) – is derived from Mughal buildings of the 17th century but in a style by this time prevalent in the Deccan. The recent restoration of the buildings was supported by the U.S. Ambassador's Fund for Cultural Preservation.

Tomb of Mah
Laqa Bai Chanda

PAGE 66
Shrine of Maula
'Ali, interior

See photo on page 13

The tour described in this volume continues with Golconda, the fortified city that preceded Hyderabad as capital of the region. Golconda consists of three connected but separate fortified areas, known respectively as the Bala Hisar (Lofty Citadel), the Outer Fort and the Naya Qil'a (New Fort), built in stages between the 14th and 17th centuries. Clustered within the walls of the Bala Hisar are several courtly buildings, while the Outer Fort contains mosques, shops, and residences built as the city expanded from its original core. In the Naya Qil'a, constructed in about 1656 as a defense against the Mughal armies, are two mosques, as well as the remains of a garden and its pavilions. Surrounding the fort are various other complexes and buildings, including tombs, caravanserais and mosques; visitors must also imagine the suburbs of this royal city surrounding the fort, and continuing especially along the highway east to the port of Masulipatnam. Today the Bala Hisar comes under the protection of the Archaeological Survey of India, which charges an entrance fee. The rest of the fort may be freely explored.

BALA HISAR

The original fort of Golconda was built sometime in the 13th or early 14th century, and these early foundations are still seen on the rugged granite hill known as the **Bala Hisar**. Two sets of walls encircle the highest part of the citadel, and a third set extends down and around a small area of the flat ground to the east. The outline of this third set of walls can only partially be traced, because the palaces of the Qutb Shahi sultans were later built in this area, and parts of the old wall were demolished to accommodate them.

To identify Golconda's oldest **Walls** several distinguishing features can be noted. The walls are constructed from blocks of granite joined together without mortar; the blocks conform to the contours of the natural large boulders that cover the hill; and on many of the blocks can be found lines of rectangular holes, where metal or wooden wedges were inserted to split the blocks from the larger rock face. Several boulders on the citadel, from which blocks were evidently quarried to construct the wall, are marked with matching rows of holes for wooden wedges, which helped split the rock. The bastions in these walls also have a distinctive appearance: they are rectangular with sharply angled corners, tapering profiles, and bases wider than their apexes.

PAGES 68-69
Engraving of Golconda tombs (Louis Rousselet, *L'Inde des Rajahs, Voyage dans l'Inde Centrale*, Paris, 1875, fig. 4)

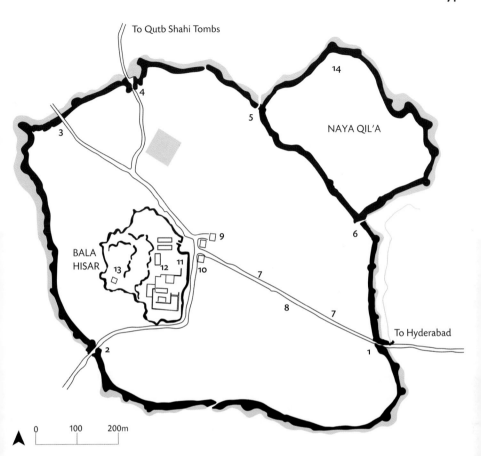

To Qutb Shahi Tombs

NAYA QIL'A

BALA HISAR

To Hyderabad

0   100   200m

GOLCONDA

1 Fateh Darwaza
2 Mecca Darwaza
3 Pattancheru Darwaza
4 Banjara Darwaza
5 Jamali Darwaza
6 Moti Darwaza
7 Bazaar Street
8 Khazana
9 Jami Masjid
10 Habshi Kamans
11 Bala Hisar Darwaza
12 Qutb Shahi Palaces
13 Baradari
14 Mosque of Mullah Khiyali

Bala Hisar, view of citadel

By following the walls with these features down the sides of the Bala Hisar, visitors can find remains of the third enclosure, and one of the original gates of the fort, now sandwiched behind a rectangular water reservoir (inside the fort) and several houses (outside the gate). Its lintel is carved with rampant elephants; the theme of battling animals is to be seen on many other fortification gates of the period, and is repeated in later gates at Golconda itself.

After the 1360s, when Golconda became part of the Bahmani sultanate, some basic changes were made to the site. It is possible that

the east-facing gate in the second set of walls was built at this time, its structure matching that of 14th-century Bahmani gates at other forts in the area. Remains of another building, once partially preserved on the ascent to the Bala Hisar, also had stucco-work like that found in buildings of the Bahmani era in other forts, and so may also connect it to this era. Because it remained a purely defensive structure, although a strategically important one, it is likely that not much more was done to develop the site, and the functional structures that once served the fort are now mostly gone.

HYDERABAD, GOLCONDA

Much more development took place in the 16th and 17th centuries, when control of Golconda passed from the Bahmanis to their governor Sultan Quli Qutb al-Mulk and his descendants, the Qutb Shahi sultans. As independence from the Bahmanis was gradually established, the Qutb Shahis built ever larger monuments at the site and constructed the ceremonial and palatial residential structures befitting a flourishing kingdom and its capital. At this time, the palace area at the base of the Bala Hisar was constructed, several mosques were founded, and tombs were built in an area north of the fort reserved for the sultans, their families and for esteemed members of the court. The earliest palace structures seem to be those nearest the base of the Bala Hisar on the south side, and in the middle of the east side. As additional palace buildings were erected, the complex expanded further to the east, necessitating the removal of the early 14th-century wall.

To see this part of the fort today, taxis, rickshaws and buses drop off visitors near the **Habshi Kamans**, two large, matching ceremonial portals probably dating to the mid-16th century. Named after the Abyssinian guards said to have been stationed there, these portals controlled access to the royal zone of the Bala Hisar. Remnants of the

OPPOSITE, TOP
Aerial view of the Qutb Shahi Palace

OPPOSITE, BOTTOM
Habshi Kamans

BELOW
Habshi Kamans, plaster detail

Jami Masjid, entrance

stuccowork show an array of beasts including fish, eagles, lions, and elephants, as well as delicate winged angels.

Tucked behind the northern arch is the earlier **Jami Masjid** (congregational mosque). This was founded by Sultan Quli in 1518, at the moment when he was elevated from being a Bahmani subordinate and his capital required a place of worship commensurate with its new status. The mosque is still in use, and although visitors are sometimes not permitted to enter they may be able to see the gate into the mosque's courtyard and the doorway built with temple spolia. The doorway is of a type common to Kakatiya temples of the 12th-13th centuries, with three bands of decoration showing pilasters, spiraling vegetation and diamond motifs. The panels below the jambs would have been carved with guardian figures, but these figures were probably erased when the doorway was placed in the mosque because they would have been inappropriate in this setting.

Why the doorway of a temple would have been removed to Golconda at this time is hard to say. It is tempting to look to events in 1530-31 when, after the successful conclusion of a campaign against Vijayanagara, Sultan Quli ordered the destruction of a temple at the fort of Devarkonda southeast of Golconda, and possibly ordered its doorway to be brought to his capital. Above the doorway is the inscription commemorating the foundation of the mosque and identifying Sultan Quli as its patron. The prayer hall on the western side of the courtyard

is quite small and simple, with 15 domed bays. The *mihrab* in the centre of the *qibla* wall, giving the direction of Mecca to the west, consists of a shallow niche framed by an ogival arch. Within the *mihrab* is a plaque inscribed with Chapter 3, Verses 33-34 of the Qur'an; above it is a stepped frame, in which the names of Allah, Muhammad, Abu Bakr, 'Umar, 'Uthman, 'Ali, Hasan and Husain have recently been painted.

Bala Hisar Darwaza

Visitors should then proceed into the Bala Hisar. The main path leads from the **Bala Hisar Darwaza** (Citadel Gate), probably part of the mid-16th century expansion of the site, into a large courtyard. In the Qutb Shahi period this was likely the public zone of the palace area, where grand audiences and larger ceremonies were held. To the right is a *hammam* (bath), now closed to visitors, and to the left is a multi-story structure called the Silah Khana (armoury), because stores of cannons, cannon balls and weapons were found there in the 19th century. Largely inaccessible today, and with several phases of additions, the Silah Khana was probably a palace when originally built; on its opposite, southern side, porticoes overlook a deep water reservoir. To the north of this area extends a garden.

Several other functional structures face this courtyard, many probably built in the late 17th century and later after the fall of the Qutb Shahi dynasty, when ceremonial use of the fort had ceased and it had returned to its purely defensive state. These include the lines of arched, open-sided rectangular buildings flanking the path to the stairs

Bala Hisar Darwaza, detail

ascending the Bala Hisar, and obscuring access to the smaller structures including a small mosque and a building, possibly a kitchen, with domes perforated with small holes.

Most visitors to the Bala Hisar during the 16th-17th centuries would have concluded their business in this part of the fort. Those of higher rank at court, though, would have proceeded south to the increasingly private zones of the palace area, where courtyard after courtyard opened to view as they moved into the heart of the palace where the sultan and his family lived. One 16th-century visitor to Golconda, the Bijapur courtier Rafi al-Din Shirazi, in fact described several enclosed areas here, including the royal residence and wardrobe, zones for the fort's commander and court ministers, and workshops for calligraphers and bookmakers.

If visitors continue to the south, rather than ascending the Bala Hisar, they will pass on their right the remains of several buildings with tripartite layouts, each with a central rectangular platform with enclosed chambers on either side. The central platform is usually reached by short sets of stairs at its ends; its rear wall is typically decorated with three arched frames into which tiers of smaller arched niches are set. This platform was probably covered by a timber roof supported on wooden columns, the stone bases for which can still be seen, though no

Taramati Mosque

such columns or roofs survive today. These tripartite buildings were typically placed around the sides of an open courtyard, as is the case here.

Moving south again, another grassy square opens up. On their right visitors will pass by the **Taramati Mosque**, fancifully named for a concubine of Sultan Abdullah Qutb Shah, and of interest for its fine plaster decoration. On the south side is a rectangular palace building, which has been extensively renovated, with crude additions obscuring the fine work of the original structure beneath. Originally it must have consisted of a central rectangular forecourt recessed from the front of the building, with octagonal rooms on either side at a higher level. These rooms are intricately decorated; some also have small fountains and toilets tucked discreetly into the corners.

Next to this building is a series of halls, now all joined, that lead to the southern end of the palace area. Upon exiting this area, visitors will be in a paved courtyard with an octagonal fountain called the **Rani Mahal** (Queen's Palace). On the east, south and west sides are buildings with the tripartite layouts described above, consisting of a central rectangular platforms with enclosed chambers on either side. Some imagination, however, is required to see this basic design in those buildings now missing many elements.

Further south, enclosed within tall walls, is a multi-chambered, open-air structure that once stood on a high platform. This had a series of rooms that opened into one another, and to the exterior, through large arched openings. The walls of this building are constructed of plaster over a combination of stone (for the walls) and brick (around the arches), with the substructure in stone. It is unclear what the function of this building was. Terracotta pipes embedded in the corners of the walls suggest that it was provided with running water, but although hydraulics and raised floors accommodating a hypocaust system are typical of baths, the large openings in the walls of this building make such identification unlikely. Other dilapidated structures can be glimpsed nearby, though most of them are inaccessible to visitors. Some of these buildings had upper storeys with scenic balconies overlooking the palace area.

To ascend the **Bala Hisar**, visitors must take the stairs at the north end of the palace area. They will pass through a breech in the early walls of cyclopean masonry, past water reservoirs and storage buildings, a Hindu shrine (recently expanded, and not original to the site), to the

OPPOSITE
Palace, interior chamber

BELOW
Palace, Rani Mahal

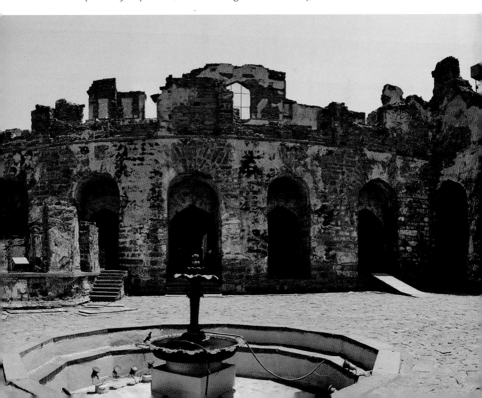

Mosque at the
top of Bala Hisar

summit where a sizeable pavilion stands. Stairs on the east side of this
pavilion lead back down to the southern end of the palace area. It seems
likely that during the 16th century this acropolis did not house buildings
for the everyday functioning of the court, but just pleasure pavilions
enjoyed in private moments. In the mid- to late 17th century when
the kingdom was under siege this part of the citadel assumed a more
functional role.

    Along the way to the top of the Bala Hisar visitors will pass
a building identified as the **Ambar Khana** (grain house) from an
inscription inside it recording its construction in 1642 by a minister
of Abdullah Qutb Shah. That inscription is now displayed in front of
the building.

    Directly above the granary, but reached by continuing up the
path, is a small **Mosque** attributed to Ibrahim Qutb Shah on the basis of
the design of its façade. However, its parapet and tall, tapering minarets
are typical of later Qutb Shahi buildings, perhaps of the mid-17th century

rather than Ibrahim's time. But the pilasters supporting the *mihrab* arch are more like features of mihrabs of the Bahmani era, so it seems likely that the mosque was originally built in the 14th century, and the minarets and eaves added later.

At the summit of the Bala Hisar is a **Baradari** commanding magnificent panoramas of the whole fort, including the palace below and the Qutb Shahi tombs in the far distance. Though the term *baradari* usually refers to a 12-arched garden pavilion, after years of changes, the building no longer matches the type after which it is named. Now, there is a lower story, whose original facade of arches resting on faceted columns can be glimpsed behind walls several metres thick built in front. Behind are several rooms and stairs leading up to a second story with a pavilion overlooking the palace area on the east, and the surrounding countryside on the west. On the roof of the *baradari* is a structure often described as a throne, where presumably the sultan sat to enjoy the views and refreshing breezes.

Baradari at the summit of Bala Hisar

See also photo on pages 8-9

OUTER FORT

Golconda's outer fort was built in the 1550s, after the Qutb Shahi realms had suffered various invasions, and the population of the capital, now expanded beyond what could be safely contained within the early walls, was endangered. An inscription in the outer fort's Mecca Darwaza commemorates the completion of the construction in 1559.

In comparison with the earlier walls of the Bala Hisar, the 16th-century **Walls** are characterized by regularly-shaped, square granite blocks set in even courses and bonded with mortar. The tops of the walls are in most places capped with a horizontal course of finely worked reddish stone and large rounded merlons with machicolations at regular intervals. Bastions are round or polygonal, and there are no prominent tool marks, as on the 13th-14th-century walls.

Each of the eight gates into the Outer Fort is slightly different in style, suggesting that the walls may have been built in sections by different groups of laborers. Some of the gates, such as the **Pattancheru and Banjara Darwazas**, both on the northwest side of the Outer Fort, have panels carved with animals in a fashion similar to the gates of the Bala Hisar described above.

See photo on page 3

A **Bazaar Street**, more than 500 metres long, was then built to connect the Bala Hisar Darwaza and the palace area with the Fateh Darwaza of the Outer Fort. This was the primary entrance to the fort from the road leading east from Golconda to Hyderabad and on to the port of Masulipatnam. It seems probable that the Habshi Kamans at the head of the street, already described, were also added at this time. Lining the street are a variety of buildings dating from the mid-16th to late 17th centuries. The shops here are thought to have been built by

LEFT
Banjara Darwaza

RIGHT
Banjara Darwaza, fortified entry

Khairat Khan, the minister who also built the Ambar Khana on the Bala Hisar, because an inscription (now mounted near these structures) states that in 1640 he built stores, a well and a garden at the fort.

A building near the shops, called the **Khazana** (treasury), now serves as an archaeological museum housing assorted sculptures. It too appears to have been constructed in the 17th century, but it is unknown if its original function was as a storeroom. The building consists of rooms with arched openings facing a central courtyard, with an *iwan* (vaulted room) open on one side in the middle of the side facing the entrance. A caravanserai is another possible identification.

Throughout the rest of the Outer Fort there must have been many other buildings, such as residences, mosques, bath and shops, that served the neighborhoods of this capital city. This part of the fort is still occupied, though, and very little of that history survives aside from the 1667-68 **Hira Masjid** in the former diamond-merchants' quarter. This mosque is set within a walled enclosure entered through a gate on the east side. The front of the prayer hall is now obscured by a concrete extension, but its upper elevation is still visible. In the spandrels of the three arches of its facade are calligraphic medallions, and the mosque's dedicatory inscription is in the cornice above this, written on panels between stone brackets with pendant lobes.

ABOVE
Banjara Darwaza, wooden door

BELOW
Bazaar Street

NAYA QIL'A

See photo on page 1

The **Naya Qil'a** appendage to the northeast side of Golconda's Outer Fort was likely built by Abdullah just after a 1656 Mughal siege of the fort led by Aurangzeb. According to the Mughal chronicle, the *Ma'asir-i 'Alamgiri (Glories of 'Alamgir [Aurangzeb])*: "Before his accession to the throne [in 1658] when Aurangzeb invaded this country but afterwards graciously pardoned Abdullah Qutb-ul-Mulk, he, in the thought that Aurangzeb might return, built a strong fort round this hillock and included it within the fort of Golconda, and thus gained security." (Translation by Jadunath Sarkar, Calcutta: Royal Asiatic Society of Bengal, 1947, p. 183).

The 17th-century walls enclosed an area that had been developed beforehand. Among the earlier buildings are the **Mosque of Mullah Khiyali**, dating to 1570, and, near a massive baobab tree, the **Mosque of Mustafa Khan**, constructed in 1560 as indicated by an inscription panel above the door into its courtyard. The 1560 mosque stands on a broad rectangular platform with a courtyard preceding it. The courtyard, enclosed by a tall wall lined on both inner and outer sides by a row of blind arches, holds the beautifully inscribed graves of Mustafa Khan, a minister to Ibrahim Qutb Shah, and other family members. The *mihrab* in the prayer hall has bold, swooping calligraphy arranged free-form around the arch, which is unusual for Qutb Shahi mosques.

Possibly during the reign of Abdullah, a garden was laid out near these two mosques. It originally had a formal plan with a 180-metre long water channel that ran from north to south through its centre. This channel was once lined with inclined stone slabs that caused the water flowing over them to break into gentle ripples. A row of pavilions and step-wells, and an aqueduct that passed over the eastern wall of the fort create a shorter east-west axis perpendicular to the water channel.

The entire area was then enclosed with stone walls by order of Abdullah, with numerous bastions outfitted with cannons. Most unusual is the east-facing **Nine-lobed Bastion**. To much protest and consternation, the Naya Qil'a was recently leased to the Hyderabad Golf Association and part has been turned into a golf course. While the mosques and fort walls have been protected, it appears that the few remaining traces of the 17th-century garden are fast disappearing.

Mosque of
Mullah Khiyali,
with baobab tree

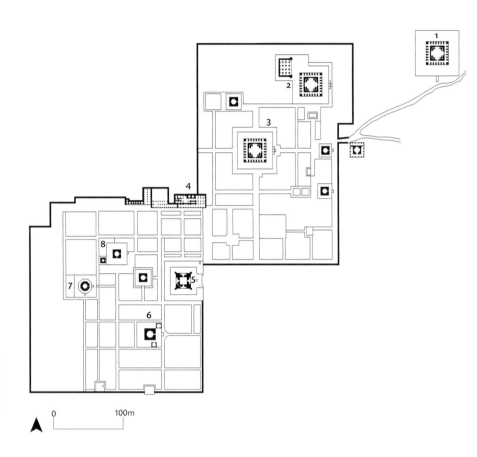

GOLCONDA TOMBS

1 Tomb of Abdullah Qutb Shah (d. 1672)
2 Tomb and Mosque of Hayat Bakhshi Begum (d. 1667)
3 Tomb of Muhammad Qutb Shah (d. 1626)
4 *Hammam*
5 Tomb of Muhammad Quli (d. 1612)
6 Tomb of Ibrahim (d. 1580)
7 Tomb of Jamshid (d. 1550)
8 Tomb of Sultan Quli (d. 1543)

HYDERABAD, GOLCONDA

QUTB SHAHI TOMBS

The tombs of the Qutb Shahis are located to the north of the Outer Fort, reached by passing through the Banjara Darwaza. All the sultans are buried here except the last, Abu'l Hasan, who was interred in Daulatabad where he was held prisoner by the Mughals after being captured during the conquest of Golconda in 1687. The first tomb built at the site was for Sultan Quli (d. 1543), founder of the Qutb Shahi dynasty, and his monument came to be surrounded by the tombs of his descendants, their wives and children, as well as a few of the important courtiers of the 16th and 17th century.

Visitors now approach the site from the east and enter through a wall erected in the early 20th century in order protect the tombs, though several small mosques and tombs now fall outside of that enclosed zone. The wall also leads from the later monuments to the earlier monuments, now at the back of the enclosed area, thereby obscuring the original situation of the tombs. These had been carefully oriented to Golconda's Outer Fort, and were once approached from the Pattancheru Darwaza rather than the modern road to the east.

Sultan Quli's tomb, one of the smallest at the site, is raised on a relatively low platform. Other important mausoleums are the

Tomb of Muhammad Quli

Tomb of Ibrahim (d. 1580), with a square exterior, once tiled; the **Tomb of Muhammad Quli** (d. 1612), with unique columned porches; the **Tomb of Muhammad** (d. 1626) with traces of green tilework; the **Tomb of Hayat Bakhshi Begum** (d. 1667), interred in one of the larger tombs at the site; and the **Tomb of Abdullah** (d. 1672), her son, constructed at the peak of the tomb-building tradition. These and many of the other tombs can be been identified by inscription on the gravestones set into the ground in the substructure of the building, or on the stone cenotaphs within the domed chambers above.

The one mystery of the complex is where the second Qutb Shahi sultan was buried; although the octagonal tomb near Sultan Quli's tomb is identified as the **Tomb of Jamshid** (d. 1550), it has no inscribed cenotaph, and instead has two large female gravestones and one small male gravestone inside. The decorative features of this building are closer to those found in 17th-century buildings, and it is likely that this building, associated with Jamshid only within recent years, was in fact intended for someone else. Also buried in the royal necropolis are ministers and others associated with the court, including the courtesan Pemamati, a favorite of Abdullah.

As visitors will note, the later monuments are larger than the earlier ones, and they stand on higher platforms so that they appear even more imposing. This variation reflects the changes in the dynasty's status and wealth over time, from the reign of Sultan Quli, who professed obeisance to the Bahmanis, to the era of the later sultans who ruled over a fully independent realm with its own international connections. The features of the buildings also evolved with time. While most are cubical chambers with facades articulated by arched recesses and crowned with bulbous domes on petalled bases, other architectural flourishes are unique to the moment in which they were built. The faceted stone columns on Muhammad Quli's tomb, for instance, can also be found on other buildings of the era, and the massive construction of Abdullah's and Hayat Bakhshi Begum's tombs is matched by the equally massive construction in contemporary palaces, which also have metre-thick walls and large vaulted spaces.

ABOVE
Tomb of Jamshid

OPPOSITE
Tomb of Muhammad Qutb Shah

See also photos on pages 14 and 15

Decades of restorations have altered the exterior appearance of most of the structures, but it is still possible to trace the evolution of stucco decoration from the simple forms on Sultan Quli's tomb to the more elaborate work on the **Tomb and Mosque of Hayat Bakhshi Begum** (d. 1667), where bands of floral design outline each arch and scrolling ribbons rest atop their apexes. Tiles are partially preserved on only one side of Ibrahim's tomb and in very small patches on Muhammad and Abdullah's tombs, but these were likely a significant aspect of the decorative program of the buildings, a fact also mentioned by Thèvenot. Also notable are the dark black basalt grave markers with calligraphy and other beautifully carved details in each tomb.

ABOVE
Mosque of Hayat Bakhshi Begum, plaster detail

LEFT
Mosque of Hayat Bakhshi Begum

Several water tanks, some with subterranean chambers, a *hammam* and a caravanserai can also be found in this area. The caravanserai is now hidden in overgrowth and behind a locked gate, with only the top part of a mosque visible, but an earlier view of the area shows a rectangular walled area divided into courtyards surrounded by arched porticos, where travellers could store their goods and rest for the night. The **Hammam** on the southern side of the caravanserai is now commonly identified as a mortuary bath, in which to prepare the dead bodies before their internment, but more likely served those staying at the caravanserai or living in this area outside of the fort. The entrance to the *hammam* is into a room with elevated platforms around

Hammam in the tomb complex, interior

a small fountain, and an oculus above. This leads into an antechamber with toilets on one side, and a room with a water storage tank on the other. The large room opening from the antechamber is dominated by a low 12-sided platform with swirling, black basalt stripes, presumably used for massaging.

A small museum is also located on the south side of the caravanserai. In it are displayed some manuscripts, mostly Qur'ans, as well as pottery and arms found at the site. Behind the mosque of Muhammad Quli is an **'Idgah** (open-air space for performing prayers on the Muslim holidays of Eid al-Fitr and Eid al-Adha). The carved decoration that can be seen through the layers of whitewash appears similar to that on Golconda's Jami Masjid, suggesting that the *'idgah* was constructed during the reign of Sultan Quli.

The tombs have recently been restored by the Aga Khan Trust.

AROUND GOLCONDA

Scattered around the walls of Golconda's Outer Fort are a number of buildings worth visiting. **The Sheikhpet Sarai** is a caravanserai located about 1,000 metres north of the Qutb Shahi tombs, currently under restoration. The walls enclose a tomb, a mosque and several other utilitarian structures. The mosque here has an inscription of 1633-34 during the reign of Abdullah. The tomb no longer has its inscription to help identify its builder, but the panel above the door where it was once affixed is evident. It is a square, flat-roofed structure with faceted columns, like those of the tomb of Muhammad Quli, but this building is entirely stone, and the porticoes run along all four sides. Traces of lovely Qutb Shahi stone carving can still be seen, notably on the roundels on the facade of the mosque, with mirror calligraphy.

To the southwest of the Outer Fort, in an area thought to have been the site of a royal garden, the **Taramati** *Baradari* sits atop a hill overlooking the surroundings. The building is named for a consort of Sultan Abdullah Qutb Shah; whether or not a connection can be made to her, the structure is a good example of 17th-century architecture, with the same massive structure and arch-net vaulting seen in some of the buildings in the palace area. Since 2004, the Andhra Pradesh State Tourism Department has run a restaurant here, and it also hosts dance and musical performances.

A short distance away, also set picturesquely atop a hill, is the so-called **Mosque of Pemamati**, another of Abdullah's favourites. Its

LEFT
'Idgah in the tomb complex

RIGHT
Sheikhpet Sarai

facade of carved stone reflects 17th-century developments in mosque architecture, with eaves supported by decorative brackets over a row of simple arches. Its corner towers, never finished, would have added height and grandeur to the whole composition.

On the road leading from Golconda to Hyderabad is the **Toli Mosque**. It is one of many monuments once lining this thoroughfare, and visitors can find several other mosques, tombs and structures of the era by walking through this area called Karwan (Caravan). The Toli Mosque was erected in 1671 by Musa Khan, chamberlain of Abdullah, and its decoration shows how the mosque of Pemamati would have looked if completed. Tall corner minarets rise for several storeys above stone bases, ending in proportionately small domed finials resting on a fringe of petals. Scrolling stucco designs adorn each arch of the façade; above the eaves are further arches with pierced screens of a variety of geometric designs. Much impressive stuccowork is also preserved inside, including a *mihrab* with dedicatory inscription, calligraphic roundels in the spandrels of the arches, and the unusual feature of miniature facades of the mosque replicated on the *qibla* wall at the end bays. These elements are combined with simply carved stonework.

GOLCONDA

TRAVELLERS' ACCOUNTS

Description of Golconda by Abbé Carré, sent from France to report on the diplomatic progress of the French East India Company, in India between 1672 and 1674.

I had myself carried in my palanquin, disguised as a Persian merchant, sometimes to Golconda and other times to Baghnagar [Hyderabad]. These are two powerful and opulent towns, half a league from one another, and the capitals of this rich kingdom of Golconda. The first, which gives its name to the kingdom, is called royal, as the king generally lives here. It is situated partly in a valley and partly on the side of a high mountain, whose summit is covered with a large castle, precipitous on all sides, difficult of access, and commanding the town. The whole place is enclosed within strong walls, which, on the side of the country, are almost all surrounded by large ditches, formerly full of water, but now half filled with mud, bog and earth, dried by the heat of the sun. Many bastions face the side of the country but these are more remarkable for their antiquity than for their strength, being now only an ornament to the walls, which are about a league in circumference, surrounding the town and mountain. Inside them lie only the king's palace and his magnificent seraglio, with the mansions of the princes and the houses of all the nobility and officers of the court.

It was a great pleasure and most interesting each morning to watch the pomp and magnificence of the princes and nobles of this place, who display their riches, jewels and precious stones, to excite the envy of the others. Some adorn their elephants; some the harness of their horses and their arms; while others decorate their palanquins with rich ornaments, and above all wear splendid clothes, which lend great brilliance to their assemblies. I avow that I passed some agreeable hours in watching all this splendour of the Golconda court...

From *The Travels of the Abbé Carré in India and the Near East, 1672 to 1674*. Translated by Lady Fawcett, edited by Sir Charles Fawcett and Sir Richard Burn (London: Hakluyt Society, 1947), pp. 327-29.

Description of Golconda by Thomas Bowrey, an independent trader who was in India between 1669 and 1688.

The Faire and Beautifull Citty of Golcondah is an inland one and the Metropolitan of the Kingdome, the Residence of the Kinge and Queen, and many Lords, and of most of the forces of the Whole Kingdome. It is a Citty of very Small Antiquities, for the most part built within these 100 years past, begun when the Ancestors of the familie of this present Kinge [Abu'l Hasan Qutb Shah, r. 1672-87] revolted from the Mogull and conquered this Kingdome

...This Kingdome... hath the Enjoyment of the most plenty of rich Diamonds in the Universe. About 100 miles from Golcondah the Earth doth most abound therewith, where any Merchant adventurer may purchas a piece of land of halfe an Aker, a whole Aker or more, but at deare rates, as it Sometimes fall out. The Merchant giveinge 8, 10, 20 thousand Pagodes for a Small Spot of land, hath the liberty to digge so deep as he pleaseth, and wash out the Earth Searchinge for what hidden treasure he may happily find, but severely inspected by the King's Officers, soe that if he meet with a rough Diamond that weyeth above 70 or 72 Conderines, the Exact weight of one Royal of 8, it must be for the King's owne Use, he payinge or causinge to be paid soe much moneys for it, (but little more than one halfe the just worth) the rest of Smaller weight and magnitude are att the Adventurers owne disposal, and thus Sometimes they reape Vast Estates in Short time, and Some loose them.

Amongst the famous buildings of Golcondah may well be in the number the Mosquees and Tombs of the deceased Kings and Queens, Especially that of the last queen Mother that deceased, whose Bones, after 7 years interred were taken Up and Sent to Mecha, there againe interred in the Land of their Ungodlie Patron, the tombe of her first buriall haveinge much added to the repaire thereof, done by this King's father [Abdullah Qutb Shah], who deceased Soon after he had finished the Worke, Anno 1671. Hee caused 3 Globes of Massy Gold to be placed on the topp of the Tombe with 3 large halfe Moons of the Same. And caused the Said Tombe to be reverenced as a most Sacred Monument.

...One thinge more I must needs Mention for the honour and Praise all travellers ought to give it, (beinge what is its dessert) I meane the Kingdome in General, throughout which great care is taken both for the Safety wee Enjoy, and for relieve all travailers may have, which is first it is blessed with good and cleane Roades, and Upon Every common of above 4 or 5 miles in length, there is built a Small house or two where, if the travailer is thirsty, a thinge frequent in these warme climates, he may have milke or Congy, which is water boyled very well with Some rice in it, at the King's charge, and the people demand nothinge for it, but if any man will give them a penny or two, they have the wit to receive it very thankfully.

From *A Geographical Account of Countries Round the Bay of Bengal, 1669-79*, edited by Sir Richard Carnac Temple (London: Hakluyt Society, 1905), pp. 105-17.

TRAVELLERS' ACCOUNTS

Description of Hyderabad by Jean de Thèvenot, a French traveller who passed through the city in the 1660s.

The Palace which is three hundred and four score Paces in length, takes up not only one of the sides of the [Char Kaman plaza], but is continued to the four Towers [Charminar], where it terminates in a very lofty Pavillion. The Walls of it which are built of great Stones, have at certain distances half Towers, and there are many Windows towards the palace, with an open gallery to see the views. They say it is very pleasant within, and that the Water rises to the highest Apartments .... No Man enters into this Palace, but by an express Order from the King, who grants it but seldom ....”

From *The Travels of Monsieur de Thèvenot into the Levant, newly done out of French.* London: printed by H. Clark, 1687.

Description of Hyderabad, by the French jeweller and diamond merchant, Jean-Baptiste Tavernier, in India in the mid-17th century.

When the King sits to do justice, I observe that he comes into the Balcone that looks into the [Char Kaman plaza], and all that have business stand below, just against the place where the King sits. Between the people and the Walls of the Palace are fixed in the ground three rows of poles, about the length of a half-pike, to the ends whereof they tye certain ropes across one upon another. Nor is any person whatsoever permitted to pass beyond those bounds, unless he be called...A Secretary of State sits below the Balcone, to receive all Petitions, and he has five or six together, he puts them in a bag and then an Eunuch, who stands in the Balcone neer the King, lets down a string, to which the Bag being ti’d, he draws it up, and presents to his Majesty.

From *The Six Travels of John Baptista Tavernier, Baron of Aubonne, through Turky and Persia to the Indies during the space of Forty Years.* Made into English by J.P. (London, 1678), p.64.

The Chowmahalla Palace, described by a French officer in 1750.

[T]he fairest, the largest and the chief of all the house of this city is named the Charmahal ... It is surrounded by a wall which encloses nearly half a league in circumference. In the midst is a tank, divided into equal parts by a curtain, in which are small jets of water placed all around at distances of six feet by six. This tank is very large; about 300 jets of water are counted here, and it has a house on each face of it: the most beautiful and the largest ... is extremely large and high, from above the [dome] all the city can be seen. It is composed of living rooms, above and below, and is full of gates and windows—above which are Arabic writings in golden letters. All the huge body of the house is supported by beams of an extreme bulkiness and height.

...The other block of houses which faces this one and which is similarly on the other side of the tank ...is built on the same model as the preceding one. At the back is to be seen a curtain wherein there are cascades at regular intervals which fall into the tank. All the remainder of the Charmahal is a tract of land very fit to form a magnificent garden, but the Musalmans, lazy by nature, do not clear it.

From Jadunath Sarkar, "Haidarabad and Golkonda in 1750 as Seen through French Eyes," *Islamic Culture* (1936), pp. 234-47.

LIST OF RULERS

QUTB SHAHIS 1493-1687
Sultan Quli, 1493-1543
Jamshid, 1543-50
Subhan, 1550
Ibrahim, 1550-80
Muhammad Quli, 1580-1612
Muhammad, 1612-26
Abdullah, 1626-72
Abu'l Hasan, 1672-87

MUGHAL PERIOD 1687-1724

ASAF JAHIS 1724-1948
Qamar al-Din, Nizam ul-Mulk (1st Nizam), 1724-48
Nasir Jung, 1748-50
Muzaffar Jung, 1750-51
Salabat Jang, 1751-62
Nizam `Ali Khan (2nd Nizam), 1762-1803
Sikander Jah (3rd Nizam), 1803-29
Nasir al-Daula (4th Nizam), 1829-57
Afzal al-Daula (5th Nizam), 1857-69
Mahbub `Ali Khan (6th Nizam), 1869-1911
Mir Osman `Ali Khan (7th Nizam), 1911-48

GLOSSARY

'alam metal standards symbolizing those carried by Husain and his partisans in the battle of Karbala

'ashurkhana building where **'alam**s are displayed during Muharram

bangla a curved roof that imitated thatched buildings in Bengal; feature of 17th-century Mughal architecture

baradari 12-arched garden pavilion

cenotaph marker for a burial when the remains are located elsewhere

char/chow corruptions of the word *chahar*, meaning four

chhatri domed kiosk

Dakhni form of Urdu that developed in the Deccan

dar al-shifa literally, place of healing, a hospital

darbar court

dargah shrine around the tomb of a Sufi saint

darwaza gate or door

deori mansion

diwan prime minister

Habshi Abyssinian

hammam steam bath

haveli mansion

hisar citadel

'idgah open-air space for performing prayers on the Muslim holidays of Eid al-Fitr and Eid al-Adha

iwan vaulted room or arched portal

jali screen

Jami Masjid Friday (congregational) mosque

kalamkari dyed cotton textile

kaman literally, a bow, used as a reference to an arch

khazana treasury

khanqah Sufi retreat

mahal palace

masjid mosque

mihrab niche marking the direction of Mecca on a mosque's **qibla** wall

minar tower, minaret

muqarnas honeycomb-like structure or vaulting comprising concave elements

pul bridge

purana/purani old

qibla direction of prayer in Islam, toward Mecca

qil'a fort

tarafdar holder of a province, governor

SELECT BIBLIOGRAPHY

Bawa, V.K., *The Last Nizam: The Life and Times of Mir Osman Ali Khan*. New Delhi: Penguin Books, 1991.

Dalrymple, William, *White Mughals: Love and Betrayal in Eighteenth-Century India*. New York: Viking, 2003.

Husain, Ali Akbar, *Scent in the Islamic Garden: A Study of Deccani Urdu Sources*. Oxford and Karachi: Oxford University Press, 2000.

Khalidi, Omar, *Romance of the Golconda Diamonds*. Ahmedabad: Mapin, 1999.

----, *A Guide to Architecture in Hyderabad, Deccan, India*. 2005. (Available for download at http://dspace.mit.edu/handle/1721.1/69102)

Luther, Narendra, *Hyderabad: A Biography*. Oxford: Oxford University Press, reprinted 2012.

Lynton, Harriet Ronken and Mohini Rajan, *Days of the Beloved*. University of California Press, 1974.

Mackenzie Shah, Alison, "Nineteenth-Century Hyderabad: Re-scripting Urban Heritage", *The City in the Islamic World*. Edited by Salma K. Jayyusi, Leiden and Boston: Brill: 2008, Vol. I, pp. 589-614.

Metcalf, Thomas R., *An Imperial Vision: Indian Architecture and Britain's Raj*. Berkeley and Los Angeles: University of California Press, 1989.

Michell, George and Mark Zebrowski, *Architecture and Art of the Deccan Sultanates*. Cambridge: Cambridge University Press, 1999.

Nayeem, M.A., *The Heritage of the Qutb Shahis of Golconda and Hyderabad*. Hyderabad: Hyderabad Publishers, 2006.

Philon, Helen, ed., *Silent Splendour: Palaces of the Deccan, 14th-19th Centuries*. Mumbai: Marg Foundation, 2010.

Ramamrutham, Bharath, with Anthony Korner and George Michell, *Falaknuma, Hyderabad*. Chennai: Graf Publishing, 2010.

Safrani, Shehbaz, ed., *Golconda and Hyderabad*. Bombay: Marg Publications, 1992.

Sherwani, H.K., *History of the Qutb Shahi Dynasty*. Delhi: 1974.

Tillotson, G.H.R., "Vincent J. Esch and the Architecture of Hyderabad 1914-36", *South Asian Studies*, 9 (1993), pp. 29-46.

Vottery, Madhu, *A Guide to the Heritage of Hyderabad: The Natural and the Built*. New Delhi: Rupa Publications, 2010.

ACKNOWLEDGEMENTS

In the research and preparation of this volume, the author would particularly like to thank Sunita and Nanda Kumar Reddy, Nabiha and Humayun Mirza, Bharati and Yeshwant Ramamurthy, Anvar and Indrani Alikhan, Sunita, Roy and Roshni Verghese, Hansraj and Asha Koppada, Klaus Rötzer, Helen Philon and George Michell.

The photographs throughout the volume are by Surendra Kumar, except for those on pages 37, 74 (bottom), 76, 84 (right) and 85, which are by the author, and on those on pages 17, 19 and 26 which are courtesy of The San Diego Museum of Art. The vintage photographs on pages 10-11, 29 and 98-99 are from the collection of Clark Worswick. All the maps and site plans have been prepared for this publication by Rahul Singh.

INDEX

Page numbers in bold have illustrations

Hyderabad,
Badshahi
'Ashurkhana,
tile panel